MY FIRST
CHRISTMAS
ACTIVITY
B·O·O·K

ANGELA WILKES

DORLING KINDERSLEY
London • New York • Stuttgart

A Dorling Kindersley Book

For Sam, Rose, and Cathy

Designer Jane Bull
Photographer Dave King
Home Economist Jane Suthering

Editor Stella Love
Text Designer Martin Wilson
Managing Editor Jane Yorke
Managing Art Editor Chris Scollen
Production Paola Fagherazzi

First published in Great Britain in 1994
by Dorling Kindersley Limited,
9 Henrietta Street, London WC2E 8PS

A CIP catalogue record for this book is
available from the British Library.

ISBN 0-7513-5199-7

Colour reproduction by Colourscan, Singapore
Printed and bound in Italy by L.E.G.O.

Dorling Kindersley would like to thank the following for
their help in producing this book: Christopher Branfield,
Jonathan Buckley, Helen Drew, Cathy McTavey,
Emma Patmore, Selena Singh, and Phoebe Thoms.

CONTENTS

CHRISTMAS IN PICTURES

My First Christmas Activity Book is full of inventive ideas for things to make for the festive season. Step-by-step photographs and simple instructions show you how to create all kinds of sparkling decorations and seasonal gifts from everyday materials. There are also lots of recipes for delicious things to eat. On the opposite page is a list of things to read before you start, and below are the main points to look for in each project.

How to use this book

The things you need
All the ingredients or materials for each project are shown, to help you check you have everything you need.

Equipment
These photographic checklists show you which utensils or equipment you need for each project.

Step-by-step
Step-by-step photographs and clear instructions show you what to do at each stage of the recipe or project.

SWEET TREATS

For presents that are both scrumptious and pretty, why not make a mouthwatering array of nutty chocolate truffles and marzipan sweets? Serve them on a plate lined with shining gold paper, or wrap them in glittering boxes. The quantities given below will make about 50 large truffles and 48 marzipan sweets. Turn the page to see the finished sweets and for ideas on how to wrap them.

COOK'S TOOLS for marzipan sweets

Small bowl
Fork
Mixing bowl
Cheese grater
Wooden spoon
Sharp knife
Sieve
Teaspoon
Paintbrush

You will need

For marzipan sweets

A few drops of food colouring in each of these colours:
Orange
Red
Green
Yellow
Pink
Brown

3 drops vanilla essence

1 egg and an extra egg yolk

115 g (4 oz) caster sugar

115 g (4 oz) icing sugar

Stoned dates Dried apricots Glacé cherries

Pecan or walnut halves Cloves

225 g (8 oz) ground almonds

1 teaspoon lemon juice

COOK'S TOOLS for truffles

Rolling pin
Swiss roll tin
Medium saucepan
Plastic bag
4 plates
Wooden spoon
Sharp knife

For truffles

225 g (8 oz) digestive biscuits

115 g (4 oz) butter

Cocoa powder

Dessicated coconut

Vermicelli

1 large tin condensed milk

4 tablespoons dessicated coconut

4 tablespoons cocoa powder

Chopped nuts

26

Making the marzipan

1 Sift the icing sugar into the mixing bowl to remove any lumps. Then add the caster sugar and the ground almonds.

2 Mix the egg, egg yolk, lemon juice, and vanilla together in the small bowl. Add them to the sugar mixture and beat well.

3 Dust the table with icing sugar and gently knead the mixture until it forms a thick, smooth paste.

Stuffed fruit and nuts

1 Split the marzipan into six balls. Add a colouring to five of the balls (don't use the brown colouring) and knead it in.

2 Cut the dried fruits in half, then sandwich a coloured ball of marzipan between the halved dates, cherries, apricots, and nuts.

Marzipan fruit

1 For oranges, make balls of orange marzipan and roll them on a fine grater. Use cloves, head end out, to make the stalks.

2 Roll pieces of red and green marzipan together into balls to make apples. Push in a clove, head end first, to make a stem.

3 For bananas, roll pieces of yellow marzipan into banana shapes, then paint on fine lines with the brown colouring.

4 Roll green marzipan into tiny balls and press them together to make bunches of grapes. Push in cloves to make the stalks.

27

Things to remember

1 Read the instructions before you start and gather together everything you need. Put on an old apron or shirt.

2 Do not cook anything unless there is an adult there to help you.

3 Weigh or measure all the ingredients you need before starting to cook.

4 Always wear oven gloves when picking up hot dishes, or when putting things into or taking them out of the oven.

5 Be very careful with sharp knives and tools. Always ask an adult to help you use them.

6 When you have finished, wash up, put everything away, and clear up any mess.

The oven glove symbol
Whenever you see this symbol by a picture or instruction, it means that you should ask an adult to help you.

The final results
The final picture shows you what the finished projects should look like, making it easy for you to copy them.

Perfect presents
Many of the projects would make good presents. To find out how to wrap them, turn to pages 44 to 48.

TRUFFLES AND BONBONS
Chocolate truffles

1 Melt the butter in a saucepan over a low heat. Then remove the pan from the heat and let the butter cool a little.

2 Break the biscuits into a plastic bag and fasten it. Then roll the rolling pin over the bag, to crush the biscuits into crumbs.

3 Add the biscuits, condensed milk, cocoa powder, and coconut to the melted butter, then mix everything together.

4 Spoon the mixture into a buttered shallow tin, then spread it out and level it with a spoon. Put it in the fridge to set.

5 Cut the mixture into 4 cm squares with a knife. Then take each square and roll it into a ball between your fingers.

6 Put the cocoa, vermicelli, nuts, and coconut on separate plates. Divide the truffles into four groups. Roll each group on a different plate.

28

The finished sweets

Shiny gold paper doily

Truffle coated in chocolate vermicelli

For another gift idea, fill a transparent tube with chocolate truffles. Add a festive touch to the tubes with pieces of shiny paper and coloured ribbons.

MARZIPAN SWEETS
This tempting display of marzipan sweets is arranged on a gold paper doily decorated with diamonds of brightly coloured foil.

Cocoa-coated truffle

Nutty truffle

Coconut truffle

CHOCOLATE TRUFFLES
Put the truffles in sweet cases. For a special Christmassy effect, you could make star-shaped doilies out of shiny gold paper and arrange your truffles on them.

Gift box containing chocolate truffles and marzipan fruit

Marzipan bananas

Marzipan grapes

Marzipan orange

Marzipan-stuffed apricot

Marzipan-stuffed pecan nuts

Marzipan-stuffed glacé cherry

Marzipan-stuffed date

Marzipan apple

29

ADVENT CALENDAR

Christmas is always exciting and one of the best ways to enjoy the build-up to it is to make an advent calendar. Advent is a name for the time before Christmas and an advent calendar has a surprise door for you to open on each of the 24 days leading up to Christmas Day. Make the calendar in November so that it is ready for the 1st December. Below you can see what you need and how to make the calendar. You will need an adult's help. Turn the page to see what it will look like!

EQUIPMENT

Jar of water

Scissors

Black pen

Paintbrush

Clear tape

Pencil

Craft knife

Ruler

You will need

Thick blue paper

Poster paints

Red

Green

Yellow

White

Glue stick

Red ribbon

Thin white card

What to do

1 On blue paper measure out and draw a rectangle the size you want the advent calendar to be. Carefully cut out the rectangle.

2 Hold the piece of blue paper down on the white card. Draw around it and cut out the rectangle of white card.

3 In pencil, draw a picture with a Christmas theme on the blue paper. It is best to make the picture simple with bold outlines.

4 Paint the picture with poster paints. Paint one colour at a time and wash the brush between each colour.

5 Pencil in 24 door flaps. Make one door flap bigger than the others and write 24 on it in pen. Number the other flaps 1 to 23.

6 Lay the blue paper on top of the white card. Ask an adult to score along three sides of each door flap with the craft knife.

7 Lift the blue paper off the card and you will see the rectangles of the door flaps marked out. Paint a tiny picture in each rectangle.

8 Turn the blue paper over so that the picture is face down. Spread glue over the back of it, avoiding the door flaps.

9 Lay the white card, picture-side-down, on the blue paper, and glue them together. Make sure they match at top and bottom.

7

COUNTDOWN TO CHRISTMAS

And here is the advent calendar. On the 1st day of December, you can open the first door. Open door number two on the 2nd day of December, door number three on the 3rd, and so on until the 24th day, Christmas Eve, when you can open the biggest door. If you have brothers and sisters, take it in turns to open the doors. Behind each door there will be a surprise picture. And when there are no more doors left, you will know that it's Christmas at last!

Finishing the calendar

Cut a short piece of ribbon and tape the two ends to the back of the advent calendar to make a hanging loop, as shown.

Opening the doors

Check what the date is, then open the door with the right number on it. Carefully fold it to one side of the picture, so that it stays open.

The calendar will look more finished if you paint a border around the edge, like this.

Try painting pictures of toys, Christmas decorations, bells, a tree, and holly and ivy.

It doesn't matter where you put the doors, as long as they are spread evenly around the calendar.

Ribbon loop for hanging up the calendar

Keep the surprise pictures simple so that they stand out.

Make a big double-door for 24th December and place it in the centre of the calendar.

9

YULETIDE CARDS

One of the best things about Christmas is sending and receiving cards and it is far more fun to make your own than to buy them. With a few basic materials you can create some really original cards. Here you can see how to make a pop-up card, a collage card, and a mock parcel. Turn the page to see how to make a concertina card and to find out what the cards will look like when they are finished.

Turn the page to see how to make a concertina card

EQUIPMENT

Paintbrush

Black pen

Scissors

Pencil

Ruler

You will need

Red and green
shiny wrapping paper

Tartan ribbons

Gold and
silver stars

White card

Silver and red glitter

Blue card

Red and
black
paper

Shiny red
card

Gold paper

Cotton wool

Glue

10

Smiling snowman card

1 Cut out a rectangle of blue card. Measure halfway across it and score a line down the middle. Fold the card along the line.

2 Draw a snowman shape with glue on the front of the card and stick cotton wool to it. Then stick stars in the sky behind it.

3 Glue on a scarf made of ribbon and a hat, mouth, and nose made of red paper. Stick on black paper circles for eyes.

Pop-up reindeer card

1 Cut a rectangle of gold card. Score and fold it as before, then draw a reindeer inside the card, standing on the fold.

2 Carefully cut around the reindeer, but not around the bottom of its hooves*. Fold the card so the reindeer pops up.

3 Glue shiny red paper to half of the card. Make a tile pattern on it with glue and glitter. Add a glitter nose and a black paper eye.

Christmas parcel

1 Cut out a rectangle of red shiny card. Measure halfway across it and score a line down the middle. Fold the card in half.

2 Write a greeting inside the card. Cut out a little tag and write on it who the card is for and who it is from.

3 Tie a ribbon around the card to make it look like a parcel and tie on the tag. Fasten the ribbon with a bow.

*Ask an adult to help you do this.

11

SEASON'S GREETINGS

And here are the finished cards! You could try making some like this, or experiment with ideas of your own by changing the themes. Angels, Santa, bells, candles, and holly leaves and berries are other good subjects for cards. Don't forget to write your Christmas greeting in each card when it is finished, and to say who the card is from.

Concertina Christmas tree

1 Cut out a rectangle of white card, 20 cm by 12 cm. Score a line down the middle of the card and fold it the same as the others.

2 Cut a strip of shiny green paper, 40 cm long and 10 cm. wide. Fold it into pleats, 5 cm wide, as shown.

3 Draw half a tree on the top fold of paper. Its branches must go over the sides of the paper. Cut out the tree.

4 Open the paper out to make a row of trees. Glue the end tree to the inside of the card. Fold the other trees inside the card.

5 Cut another tree out of shiny green paper. Glue it on to the front of the card and stick on stars for decoration.

CONCERTINA CHRISTMAS TREE

Glue one Christmas tree on to the front of the card.

Gold and silver stars

Glue one end of the row of trees inside the card.

SENDING THE CARDS

Buy envelopes the right size for each card, or make them out of coloured paper. Fold the concertina Christmas tree inside the card before putting it in an envelope, and fold back the pop-up reindeer.

POP-UP REINDEER CARD

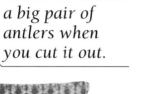

Give the reindeer a big pair of antlers when you cut it out.

Red glitter nose

Glitter glued to shiny red paper, to look like tiles

CHRISTMAS PARCEL

Tartan ribbon

Gift tag to say who the card is for and who it is from

SMILING SNOWMAN CARD

Tartan ribbon scarf

Cotton wool snow

CHRISTMAS COOKIES

This recipe is for delicious honey and spice cookies, which can be cut into festive shapes and decorated with nuts, cherries, and icing. You can buy special Christmas cutters to make the biscuits, or trace the biscuits over the page on to some card and use them as templates. The recipe makes about 36 biscuits. Turn the page for ideas on how to decorate them.

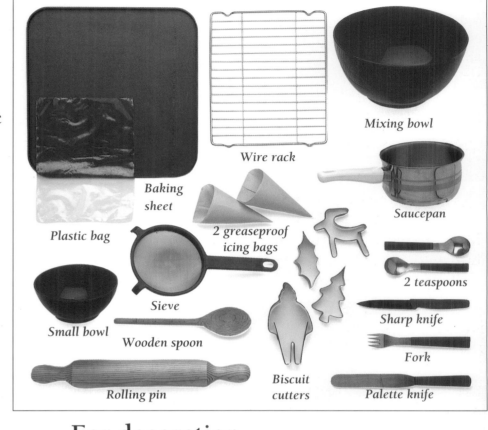

Baking sheet

Wire rack

Mixing bowl

Plastic bag

2 greaseproof icing bags

Saucepan

Sieve

2 teaspoons

Small bowl

Wooden spoon

Sharp knife

Fork

Biscuit cutters

Rolling pin

Palette knife

You will need

For decoration

340 g (12 oz) plain flour

1 teaspoon ground cinnamon

1 teaspoon ground ginger

1 teaspoon bicarbonate of soda

85 g (3 oz) dark brown sugar

A pinch of ground cloves

115 g (4 oz) butter

1 egg

4 tablespoons clear honey

1 egg white

Glacé cherries

Blanched almonds

Slivered almonds

Red food colouring

Narrow ribbons

1 teaspoon lemon juice

225 g (8 oz) icing sugar

14

Making the biscuits

1 Grease the baking sheet. Set the oven to 190°C/375°F/Gas Mark 5. Melt the butter, sugar, and honey together over a low heat.

2 Beat the egg. Sift the flour, spices, and bicarbonate of soda together, then stir in the butter mixture and the beaten egg.

3 Mix everything together, then knead it into a ball of dough. Put the dough in a plastic bag and chill it in the fridge for 30 minutes.

4 Roll the dough out on a floured table. Flour the cutter, then cut out dough shapes and place them on the baking sheet*.

5 Press cherries and nuts into some shapes. Bake the shapes for 15 minutes, until firm. Put the biscuits on a wire rack to cool.

Icing the biscuits

1 Beat the egg white in a bowl with a fork for about a minute. Sift in the icing sugar, add the lemon juice and mix until smooth.

2 For red icing, pour a quarter of the icing into a small bowl. Add a few drops of red colouring, and mix until the colour is even.

3 Spread the red icing evenly over some of the biscuits with a palette knife. Ice other biscuits with an even coating of white icing.

4 Fill one icing bag with white icing and the other with red, then carefully pipe patterns on to the finished biscuits.

* Make holes in the top of those biscuits that you want to hang up.

COOKIE COLLECTION

Decorated with nuts and cherries, and piped with white and red icing, these cookies make a stunning collection of decorations. Try making stars, bells, jolly snowmen, angels, and a bearded Santa. Thread ribbons through the hole in the top of the biscuits to hang them on your Christmas tree. You could even make a really big biscuit or two to hang on a wall, or over a mantelpiece, as a special decoration.

Blanched almond

Red ribbon

STAR OF BETHLEHEM

White piping

Glacé cherry

RED SANTA

White piping

Red icing

JOLLY SNOWMAN

Red piping

White icing

CHRISTMAS TREE

HOLLY

White piped streamers

Baubles made from dots of red piping

HEART

Slivered almonds

White piped dots

Glacé cherry

YULETIDE BELL

Red ribbon

Glacé cherries

Blanched almonds

White piping

White piping

LITTLE ANGEL

White piping

White piping

Glacé cherry

TWINKLING STAR

White piping

White piping

Red piped nose

RUDOLF

Red ribbon

SANTA'S REINDEER

CHRISTMAS NATURE TABLE

You can make wonderful Christmas decorations and presents with things that you find outdoors, in parks, woodlands, and gardens. In the autumn, start looking for interesting leaves, seedheads, and berries (check with an adult that they are not poisonous). Display them on a nature table and then, as Christmas approaches, transform them into yuletide wreaths. Here you can find out how to make different wreaths and on the next page you can see the finished results.

You will need

Dried hydrangea flowers

Red berries

Small rosehips

Red-brown leaves

Large rosehips

Blue berries

Interesting seedheads

Gold poster paint

Wide green and red ribbons

Straight twigs

Ivy leaves

Fine wire

Wreath bases

Variegated holly leaves

Plain holly leaves

Lots of spruce or fir sprigs

Evergreen leaves

Traditional wreath

1 Strip the needles from the ends of the spruce or fir sprigs. Push the ends into the wreath base to cover the top and sides.

2 Bind small bundles of berries and ivy or holly leaves together, by winding pieces of wire tightly around the stems.

3 Push the berries and leaves into the wreath base to finish the wreath, then loop a wide ribbon through the back of it.

Gilded wreath

1 Paint some ivy leaves, dried hydrangea flowers and interesting seedheads with gold poster paint and let them dry.

2 Strengthen any weak leaf or flower stems by binding a short piece of wire along each stem with a longer piece of wire.

3 Wind a broad green ribbon around a wreath base, as shown, and tie it in a big bow at the bottom of the wreath.

Christmas bundle

4 Push the golden leaves, flowers, and seedheads into the gaps between the ribbon. Arrange them to look pretty.

1 Arrange some plain twigs into a butterfly-shaped bundle. Then bind the stems of leafy twigs and red berries to the bundle with wire.

2 Tie a red ribbon around the middle of the bundle, leaving the ends loose. Then tie another ribbon around it in a bow.

FESTIVE WREATHS

Rich in colour and festive with berries and ribbons, the finished wreaths will last for several weeks, especially if they are displayed in a cool place. Just before Christmas, hang a wreath on the front door of your home as a traditional sign of welcome, or hang one at an indoor window, or above a mantelpiece as a special decoration. Try copying the wreaths shown here or create one of your own.

CHRISTMAS BUNDLE

This arrangement does not require a wreath base and can be made with any colourful leaves and berries you can find.

Dried hydrangea flowers painted gold

GILDED WREATH

Based on a simple colour scheme of green and gold, this wreath is very easy to make and makes a pretty Christmas decoration.

Gold poppy seedhead

Ivy leaves painted gold

Broad green ribbon

Twigs

Different sorts of leaves

Red ribbon

Red berries

TRADITIONAL WREATH

Using the traditional Christmas fir branches together with holly, ivy, and red berries, this wreath will look magnificent on any front door.

Red ribbon to hang the wreath

Red berries

Spruce or fir branches

Blue berries

Large rosehips

Variegated holly leaves

Ivy leaves

Small rosehips

21

CHRISTMAS SCENTS

Here you can find out how to make wonderful scented gifts for Christmas: orange and lime pomanders studded with cloves, and woodland pot-pourri – a fragrant mixture of leaves, spices, and pine cones. To allow the scents to develop, it is best to make the pot-pourri about two months before Christmas. Make the pomanders two to three weeks before you need them. Turn the page to see what they look like.

EQUIPMENT

Paper bag

Scissors

Darning needle

Sticky tape

Large jar with lid

Small bowl

Big bowl

Potato peeler

You will need

For the pomanders

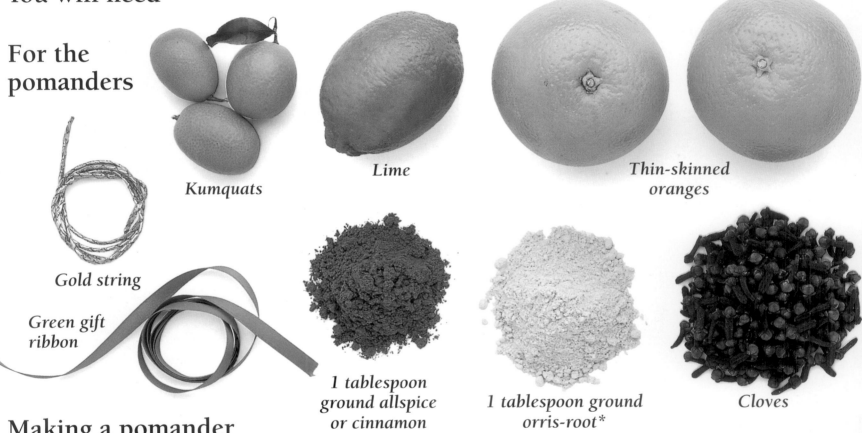

Kumquats

Lime

Thin-skinned oranges

Gold string

Green gift ribbon

1 tablespoon ground allspice or cinnamon

1 tablespoon ground orris-root*

Cloves

Making a pomander

1 Make holes in the fruit with a darning needle, then stick cloves in the holes so that the clove heads almost touch.

2 Mix the spice and ground orris-root together in a small bowl and roll the fruit in it so it is coated with the powder.

3 Tie a ribbon around the fruit. Then put the fruit in a paper bag, seal the bag with tape and leave it for two to three weeks.

* You can buy ground orris-root at herbalists, perfumers, or health food sh

For the pot-pourri

30 g (1 oz) allspice berries

1 lemon

1 orange

Fragrant sprigs of pine

1 tablespoon ground orris-root

Nutmegs

55 g (2 oz) star anise

Small pine cones

15 g (½ oz) whole cloves

1 tablespoon ground nutmeg

1 tablespoon ground cloves

1 tablespoon ground cinnamon

Cinnamon sticks

Making pot-pourri

1 A day before making the pot-pourri, finely peel off the rind of the orange and lemon and put it to dry in a warm place.

2 When the peel has dried, put all the ingredients for the pot-pourri into a bowl and mix them together well.

3 Tip the mixture into a jar, fasten the lid, and shake it. Leave it in the jar for eight weeks and shake it every day.

POT-POURRI AND POMANDERS

And here are the scented offerings. Arrange the pot-pourri in a shallow bowl or on a pretty plate, and decorate it with extra sprigs of spruce or fir. Or put it in a pot-pourri box with a decorative lid. Dust any excess spice mixture off the pomanders and tie the bows prettily around them. Arrange them around the house where you can enjoy the scent, or wrap them in tissue paper if you are giving them as presents. As the pomanders dry out, they will shrink a little, but they will keep their scent for a year or two.

MINI POMANDER

Gold string

Kumquat

Line of cloves

Pine cone

Star anise

ORANGE POMANDER

Three lines of cloves

Green satin ribbon

POMANDERS

You can make pomanders from any citrus fruit with a thin skin. Lemon skin is too thick. Why not try making mini-pomanders from kumquats, or green ones from limes, as well as the more traditional pommanders, often known as clove oranges?

Gold string

24

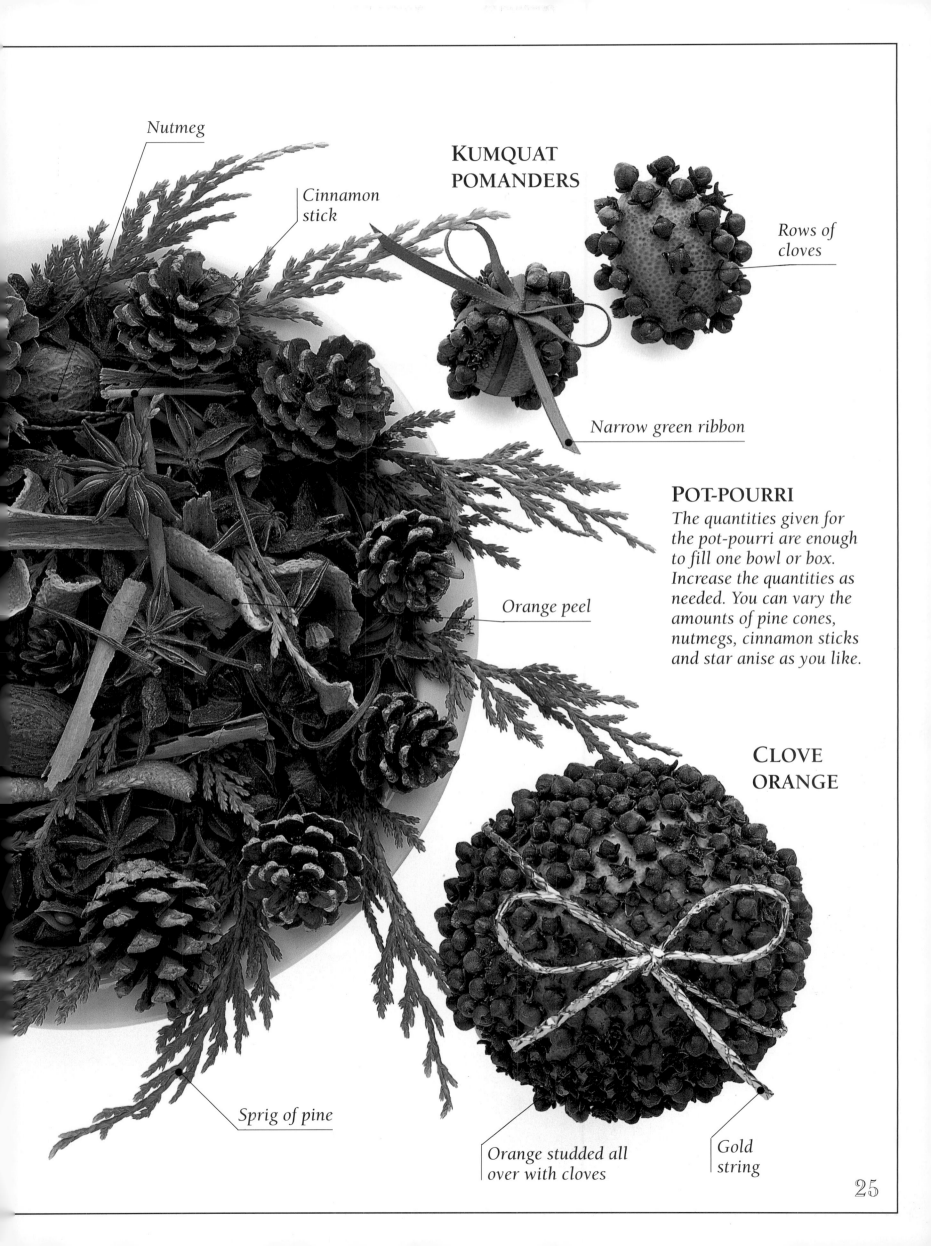

Nutmeg

Cinnamon
stick

**KUMQUAT
POMANDERS**

Rows of
cloves

Narrow green ribbon

POT-POURRI

*The quantities given for
the pot-pourri are enough
to fill one bowl or box.
Increase the quantities as
needed. You can vary the
amounts of pine cones,
nutmegs, cinnamon sticks
and star anise as you like.*

Orange peel

**CLOVE
ORANGE**

Sprig of pine

Orange studded all
over with cloves

Gold
string

25

SWEET TREATS

For presents that are both scrumptious and pretty, why not make a mouthwatering array of nutty chocolate truffles and marzipan sweets? Serve them on a plate lined with shining gold paper, or wrap them in glittering boxes. The quantities given below will make about 50 large truffles and 48 marzipan sweets. Turn the page to see the finished sweets and for ideas on how to wrap them.

COOK'S TOOLS *for marzipan sweets*

Small bowl

Fork

Cheese grater

Wooden spoon

Mixing bowl

Sharp knife

Sieve

Teaspoon

Paintbrush

You will need

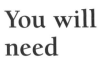

Orange

Red

Green

Yellow

Pink

Brown

For marzipan sweets

A few drops of food colouring in each of these colours:

225 g (8 oz) ground almonds

3 drops vanilla essence

115 g (4 oz) icing sugar

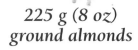

1 teaspoon lemon juice

1 egg and an extra egg yolk

115 g (4 oz) caster sugar

Stoned dates

Dried apricots

Glacé cherries

Pecan or walnut halves

Cloves

COOK'S TOOLS
for truffles

Rolling pin

Swiss roll tin

Medium saucepan

Plastic bag

4 plates
Wooden spoon

Sharp knife

For truffles

225 g (8 oz) digestive biscuits

115 g (4 oz) butter

Cocoa powder

Dessicated coconut

Vermicelli

1 large tin condensed milk

4 tablespoons dessicated coconut

4 tablespoons cocoa powder

Chopped nuts

Making the marzipan

1 Sift the icing sugar into the mixing bowl to remove any lumps. Then add the caster sugar and the ground almonds.

2 Mix the egg, egg yolk, lemon juice, and vanilla together in the small bowl. Add them to the sugar mixture and beat well.

3 Dust the table with icing sugar and gently knead the mixture until it forms a thick, smooth paste.

Stuffed fruit and nuts

1 Split the marzipan into six balls. Add a colouring to five of the balls (don't use the brown colouring) and knead it in.

2 Cut the dried fruits in half, then sandwich a coloured ball of marzipan between the halved dates, cherries, apricots, and nuts.

Marzipan fruit

1 For oranges, make balls of orange marzipan and roll them on a fine grater. Use cloves, head end out, to make the stalks.

2 Roll pieces of red and green marzipan together into balls to make apples. Push in a clove, head end first, to make a stem.

3 For bananas, roll pieces of yellow marzipan into banana shapes, then paint on fine lines with the brown colouring.

4 Roll green marzipan into tiny balls and press them together to make bunches of grapes. Push in cloves to make the stalks.

TRUFFLES AND BONBONS
Chocolate truffles

1 Melt the butter in a saucepan over a low heat. Then remove the pan from the heat and let the butter cool a little.

2 Break the biscuits into a plastic bag and fasten it. Then roll the rolling pin over the bag, to crush the biscuits into crumbs.

3 Add the biscuits, condensed milk, cocoa powder, and coconut to the melted butter, then mix everything together.

4 Spoon the mixture into a buttered shallow tin, then spread it out and level it with a spoon. Put it in the fridge to set.

5 Cut the mixture into 4 cm squares with a knife. Then take each square and roll it into a ball between your fingers.

6 Put the cocoa, vermicelli, nuts, and coconut on separate plates. Divide the truffles into four groups. Roll each group on a different plate.

The finished sweets

Cocoa-coated truffle

Nutty truffle

Coconut truffle

CHOCOLATE TRUFFLES
Put the truffles in sweet cases. For a special Christmassy effect, you could make star-shaped doilies out of shiny gold paper and arrange your truffles on them.

Gift box containing chocolate truffles and marzipan fruit

28

Shiny gold
paper doily

Truffle coated
in chocolate
vermicelli

For another gift idea, fill
a transparent tube with
chocolate truffles. Add a
festive touch to the tubes
with pieces of shiny paper
and coloured ribbons.

MARZIPAN SWEETS
This tempting display of marzipan
sweets is arranged on a gold paper
doily decorated with diamonds of
brightly coloured foil.

Marzipan
orange

Marzipan
grapes

Marzipan-
stuffed apricot

Marzipan
bananas

Marzipan-stuffed
pecan nuts

Marzipan-
stuffed glacé
cherry

Marzipan-
stuffed date

Marzipan
apple

29

CHRISTMAS TREE DECORATIONS

The Christmas tree sparkles in its place of honour, and you can make it all the more special by making your own tree decorations. Here and over the page you can find out how to make golden stars and bells, little Santas and snowmen, glistening icicles, a beaded garland, and tiny shining parcels. Start making the decorations early in December and by Christmas you'll have enough to decorate the whole tree. Turn the page to see the festive array of finished decorations.

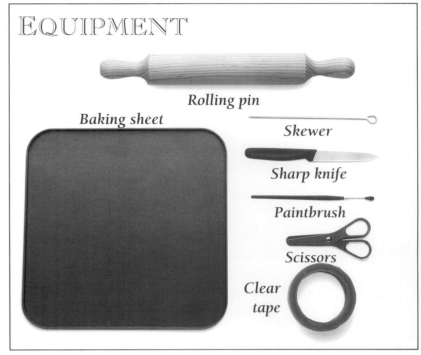

EQUIPMENT

Rolling pin

Baking sheet

Skewer

Sharp knife

Paintbrush

Scissors

Clear tape

You will need

For clay decorations

White and red oven-hardening clay

Clear varnish

Black and gold poster paint

Star and bell biscuit cutters

Narrow red ribbon

For icicles

Fuse wire

Clear plastic or glass beads

Small gold beads

For the garland

Gold poster paint

Thick red thread

Large and small red beads

Small fir-cones

Red ribbon

For shining parcels

Shiny wrapping paper

Small matchboxes

Shiny gift ribbon

Clay decorations

1 Roll out the coloured clays. Cut out red Santas, and white bells, stars, and snowmen. Make a hole in the top of each of them.

2 Add clay details to the Santas and snowmen. Then put the cut-out clay shapes on a baking tray and harden them in the oven*.

3 Let the shapes cool. Paint the bells and stars gold and finish the snowmen's faces. Then varnish the Santas and snowmen.

Sparkling icicles

 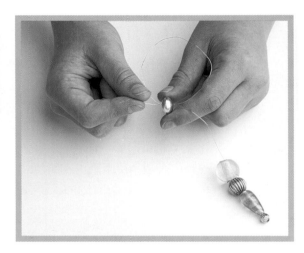 

1 Thread a gold bead on to a piece of wire and fasten it by twisting the short end of the wire back around the long end.

2 Then thread more beads on to the wire. Start with a clear bead, then a gold bead, and so on. Finish off with a gold bead.

3 Make a hanging loop above the beads and twist the end of wire below the loop to fasten it. Trim off any extra wire.

Beaded garland

1 Paint some small fir-cones with gold poster paint. Paint inside the cones as well as the outsides, then let them dry.

2 Knot one end of a long piece of thread, then thread beads on to it. At intervals, tie a fir-cone on to the thread, between the beads.

3 Fasten the end of the garland with a knot and make hanging loops at each end. Tie ribbon bows around the fir-cones.

*Ask an adult to help you harden the clay, following the instructions on the packet carefully.

A Glittering Tree

The decorations are ready and at last it is time to dress the Christmas tree. Tie each decoration firmly to a branch of the tree, making sure that each one can be seen and that you do not hang two similar things next to each other. Stand back from the tree from time to time, to check the whole effect. Hang the sparkling icicles near the ends of the boughs, where they will catch the light. Drape the beaded garland in swags from one branch to another and add the finishing touch by tying tartan bows at the tips of the branches.

Shining boxes

1 Cut out pieces of shiny paper and neatly wrap up some matchboxes containing small gifts. Tape the paper in place.

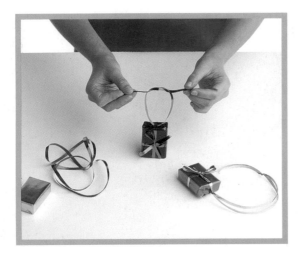

2 Tie gift ribbon around the little parcels, then tie another piece of gift ribbon through each one to make a hanging loop.

RED, GREEN, AND GOLD

Christmas trees can be a riot of differently coloured decorations, but they also work well if you restrict the colours you use. On this tree red, green, and gold have been used to create a traditional look.

Sparkling icicle

TARTAN BOWS

To make the tree look more dressy, tie short lengths of tartan ribbon in bows at the ends of the boughs.

Tartan bow

Shining parcel

Hang up the clay decorations with loops of narrow red ribbon.

Beaded garland

Yuletide bell

Smiling snowman

CHRISTMAS STOCKINGS

Why not make these decorative Christmas stockings for your family or friends? Fill them with tiny presents and hang them at the end of the bed for a Christmas Morning surprise. The amounts of felt below will make three medium-sized stockings and all their trimmings.

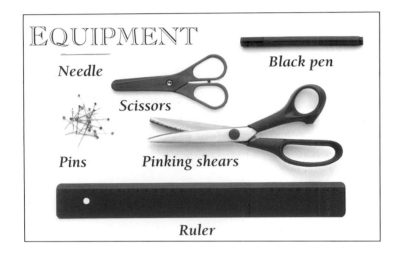

EQUIPMENT

Needle

Black pen

Scissors

Pins

Pinking shears

Ruler

You will need

50 cm squares of red, green, and white felt

Red, white, and green thread

White paper

Glue

What to do

1 Draw a stocking shape and a rectangle of the same width on the paper. Cut out the paper shapes to use as patterns.

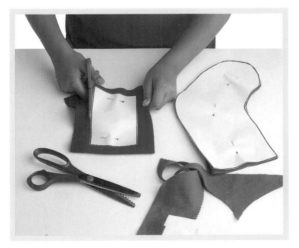

2 Pin the patterns to red and green felt and cut out two of each piece. Cut one side of the rectangles with pinking shears.

3 Pin the rectangles to the tops of the stocking pieces, as shown, and sew them together along the top edges.

34

4 Fold out the rectangular flaps. Pin and sew the two stocking pieces together round the edges, leaving the top open.

5 Turn the stocking inside out and fold the flap down. Draw designs on felt and cut them out. Cut two felt strips to make a loop.

6 Glue your felt designs to the stocking to make a picture r pattern. Glue the two strips f felt together.

WAITING FOR SANTA

Glue the double strip of felt inside the top of the stocking, to make a hanging loop. Then fill the stocking with tiny toys, sweets, or other gifts and hang it in position on Christmas Eve.

HOLLY LEAF STOCKING

SNOWY SANTA STOCKING

Red felt berries

Green felt holly leaves

Green strip cut out with pinking shears

White strips of felt glued on in a zigzag pattern

White felt beard and moustache

Red and white felt hat

White felt spots for snow

CRACKERS

Spend an afternoon with rainbow-coloured tissue paper and you can create some stunning crackers, filled with surprises, for your Christmas celebrations.

EQUIPMENT

Pencil

Scissors

Clear tape

Ruler

You will need

Shiny gift ribbon

Shiny paper

Small cardboard tubes

White card for mini-crackers

Small toys or gifts

Stencilled tissue paper (see page 44)   Plain coloured tissue paper

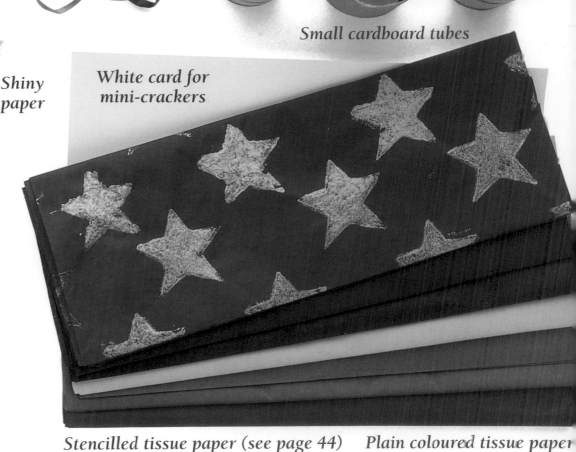

Making a cracker

1 Cut out two squares of tissue paper in different colours. Each side should be three times as long as the tube.

2 Hold the squares of paper together and cut triangles out of the top and bottom edges to make a zigzag pattern.

3 Roll up the tubes in the two pieces of tissue paper and tape the top edge down. Pinch in one end of the paper.

4 Drop a small present down inside the tube and gather in the tissue paper at the other end of the cardboard tube.

5 Cut two pieces of gift ribbon in a different colour from the cracker. Tie them in bows at each end of the cracker.

6 Cut out a strip of shiny paper. Wrap it around the middle of the cracker and tape it firmly in place.

PARTY CRACKERS

Give each person at the party a cracker to pull with a partner. Whoever gets the longest end wins the present inside!

Shiny wrapping paper cut with zigzag edges

Tissue paper printed with gold stars

Small gift

Mini-cracker made with a rolled-up tube of white card

GLOWING LANTERNS

Candles have long been associated with Christmas. Here you can find out how to create gilded lanterns using gold paper cutouts and coloured tissue paper. Stand the finished lanterns in shadowy places and ask an adult to light them for you. Then watch your lanterns glow in the dark. Remember – never leave unattended candles burning.

You will need

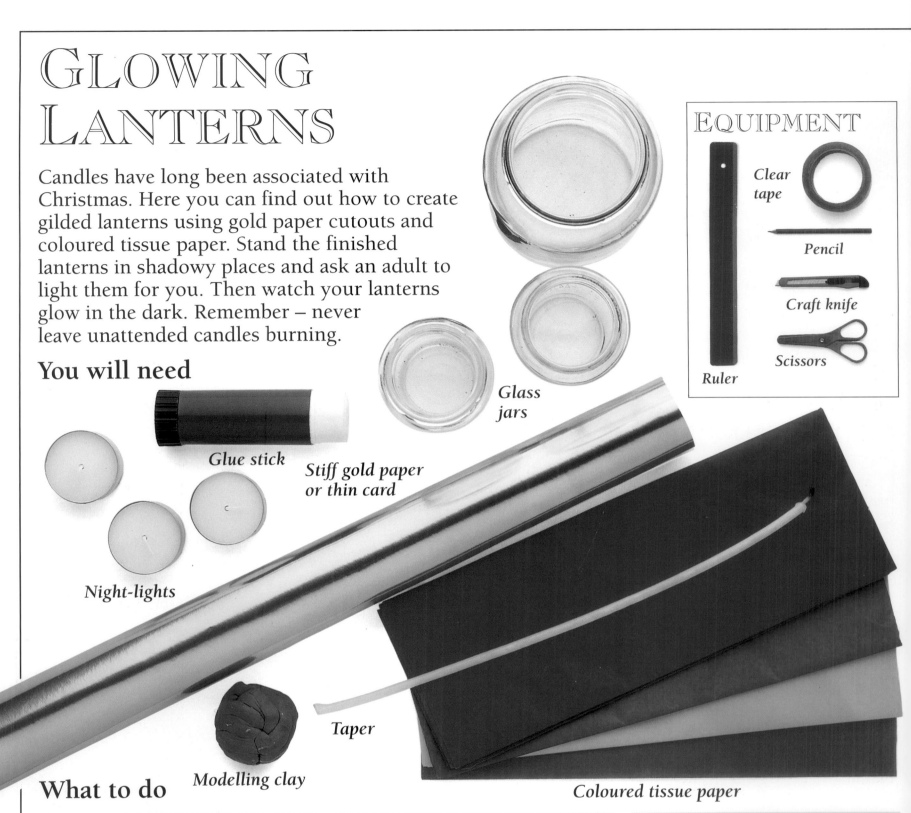

Glue stick

Stiff gold paper or thin card

Glass jars

Night-lights

Taper

Modelling clay

Coloured tissue paper

What to do

1 Make rounds of modelling clay and push the night-lights into them. Put them into the jars and press them down with a pencil.

2 To make a tree or star lantern, cut a strip of gold paper wide enough to cover a jar, and long enough to wrap around it.

3 Draw a Christmassy pattern on the back of the paper and ask an adult to help you cut out the shapes with the craft knife.

4 Tear off pieces of coloured tissue paper and glue them on the back of the gold paper, across the cut-out patterns.

5 To make the Chinese lantern, cut a strip of gold paper wider than the jar. Fold it in half and cut slits in it as shown.

6 To finish the lanterns, roll the patterned and decorated strips of gold paper around the jars and tape them in place.

LIGHTS IN THE NIGHT

Stand the lanterns in a window or on a mantelpiece. Ask an adult to light them for you, using a taper.

Gold paper with slits cut in it

CHINESE LANTERN

To make the lantern more colourful, glue tissue paper to the outside of the jar before putting the gold paper around it.

STAR LANTERN

TREE LANTERN

Zigzag edges

Cut-out triangles

Cut-out Christmas tree

Cut-out diamonds

Cut-out star

39

CHRISTMAS·TREE·CAKE

Why not make a really special cake for Christmas? This recipe is for a delicious chocolate cake that you can transform into a dazzling Christmas tree. Iced and decorated with marzipan baubles and stars, it will make a festive centrepiece for a Christmas tea. Here you can see how to make the cake and overleaf you can find out how to decorate it.

You will need

6 large eggs

90 g (3½ oz) cocoa powder

340 g (12 oz) soft margarine

340 g (12 oz) self-raising flour

1½ teaspoons baking powder

A large pinch of salt

6 drops of vanilla essence

340 g (12 oz) caster sugar

COOK'S TOOLS

25 cm square cake tin

25 cm square of greaseproof paper

Wire rack

Palette knife

Sharp knife

Wooden spoon

Mixing bowl

Making the cake

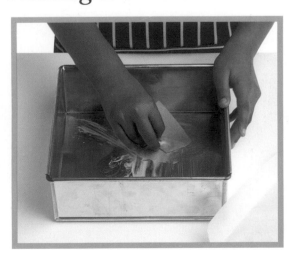

1 Set the oven to 170°C/ 325°F/ Gas Mark 3. Grease the cake tin and then line it with the square of greaseproof paper.

2 Put all the ingredients for the cake into the mixing bowl. Break the eggs into the bowl last of all.

3 Mix all the ingredients together with the wooden spoon, then beat the mixture hard for about two minutes.

4 The cake mixture should drop easily off a spoon. If it is too stiff, stir in two teaspoons of water and beat it again.

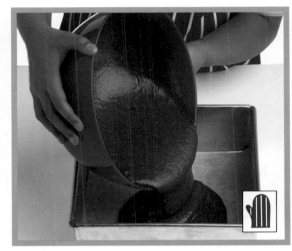

5 Pour the cake mixture into the cake tin and bake it for about 1¼ hours, until the centre feels firm and springy.

6 Let the cake cool in the tin for 30 minutes, then turn it out on to a wire rack to finish cooling and peel off the paper.

7 When the cake is cool, cut it into the pieces shown, using a sharp knife. Start by cutting the cake in half diagonally.

Cutting the cake

The different pieces of the cake are labelled to show you how to put the cake together. There are three pieces for the tree itself, two triangles for the tree's pot, two small triangles for the star on top, and two triangles for a parcel standing next to the tree.

The pieces of the cake

Tree 3

Tree 1

Star 1

Star 2

Pot 1

Pot 2

Parcel 1

Parcel 2

Tree 2

ICING THE CAKE

Once the cake is cool, you can ice it. Ice the pieces separately, then put them together on a big cake board, or board covered in kitchen foil.

COOK'S TOOLS

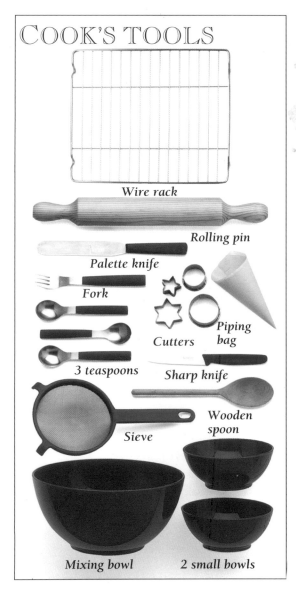

Wire rack

Rolling pin

Palette knife

Fork

Cutters

Piping bag

3 teaspoons

Sharp knife

Sieve

Wooden spoon

Mixing bowl

2 small bowls

You will need

2 teaspoons lemon juice

Yellow Red Green
food colouring

150g (5oz) marzipan

2 egg whites

450 g (1lb) icing sugar

Apricot jam

What to do

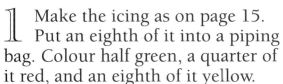

1 Make the icing as on page 15. Put an eighth of it into a piping bag. Colour half green, a quarter of it red, and an eighth of it yellow.

2 Spread green icing on all the pieces of the tree. Use red icing for the pot and yellow icing for the parcel and star.

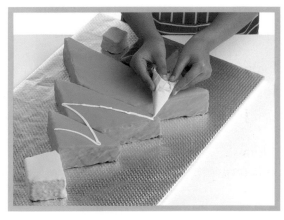

3 When the icing has set, stick the tree together with apricot jam and pipe white streamers all the way down it.

4 Colour half the marzipan red, and half yellow. Roll it out. Cut out red circles, yellow stars, and triangles for the tree's pot.

5 Decorate the tree with the marzipan shapes as shown opposite. Pipe on white dots and lines for the finishing touches.

The festive tree

And here is the finished tree! Use this picture to show you where to put the marzipan decorations, and how to ice them with the white piping. Put some of the marzipan baubles over the joins in the tree to help hide them.

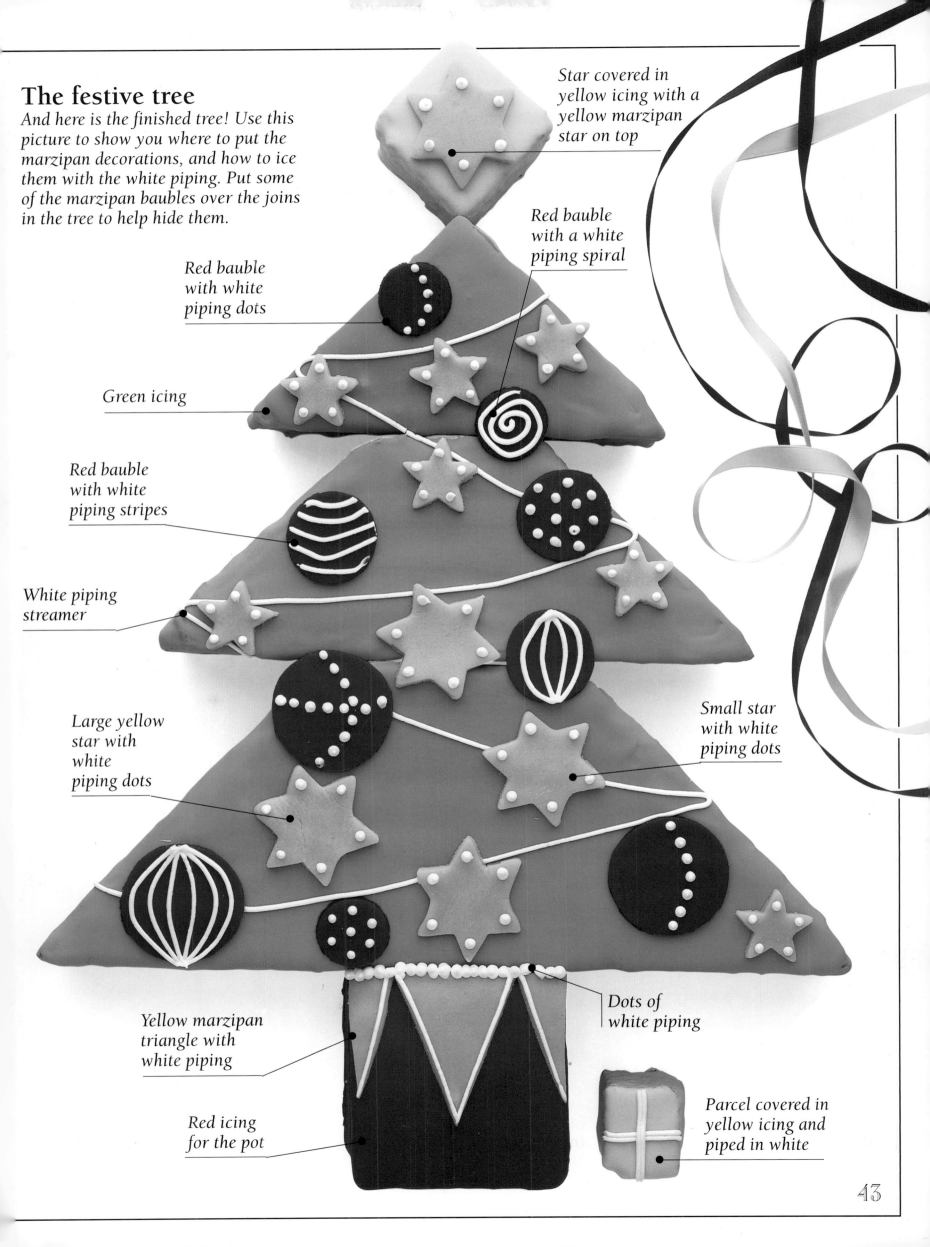

Star covered in yellow icing with a yellow marzipan star on top

Red bauble with a white piping spiral

Red bauble with white piping dots

Green icing

Red bauble with white piping stripes

White piping streamer

Large yellow star with white piping dots

Small star with white piping dots

Yellow marzipan triangle with white piping

Dots of white piping

Red icing for the pot

Parcel covered in yellow icing and piped in white

Paper Workshop

You can give your Christmas presents a really personal touch by wrapping them in paper you have printed yourself. Here you can find out how to stencil paper with gold stars and angels, create bold wax and paint prints, and make gift tags. Turn the page to see how to cover your gifts with cutouts and how to wrap differently shaped presents.

Turn the page to see how to cover your gifts with cutouts and how to wrap differently shaped presents.

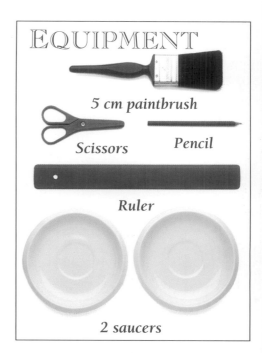

Equipment

5 cm paintbrush

Scissors *Pencil*

Ruler

2 saucers

You will need

Coloured paper

Red and gold poster paints *Sponge*

White paper

Thin white card

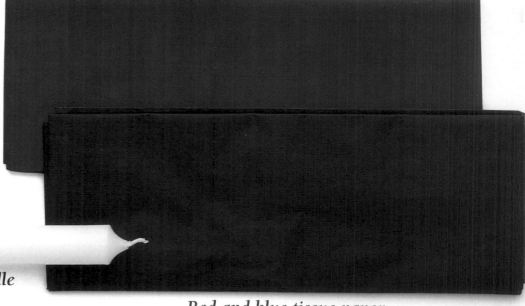

Glue stick

White candle

Red and blue tissue paper

Stencilled paper

1 To make a stencil, fold a piece of card in half. Draw half a star or angel against the folded edge and cut it out. Open the card out.

2 Pour thick gold paint in to a saucer. Hold the stencil flat on the paper. Dab the sponge in the paint, then over the stencil shape.

3 Carefully lift the stencil off the paper then repeat the stencil print all over the paper, to make a pattern. Leave the paper to dry.

Wax and paint paper

1 Draw bold patterns all over a sheet of white paper, using the white candle. Your patterns will be almost invisible.

2 Mix some paint with water in a saucer, then paint all over the paper as evenly as possible. Leave the paper to dry.

Gift tags

To make gift tags, cut and fold small rectangles of card. Glue on a square of wrapping paper, or make a stencil print on each one.

Print and paint

Gold star stencil on red paper

Gift tag to match the wrapping paper

Gold angel stencil on blue tissue paper

Wax and paint paper

Use strong colours so that the finished wrapping paper will look bold and make a striking effect.

UNDER WRAPS

The most inviting presents under the Christmas tree are those that are beautifully wrapped and tied in ribbons. Here you can find out how to wrap them and how to decorate boxes with cutouts. Turn the page to see the finished presents.

EQUIPMENT

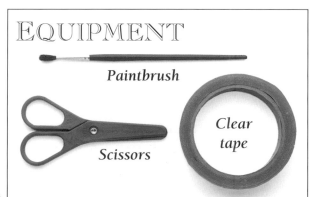

Paintbrush

Scissors

Clear tape

Colourful ribbons

Homemade wrapping paper

You will need

Pictures from colour magazines

Plain box with a lid

Glue stick

Clear varnish

Collage box

1 Cut out lots of pictures of flowers from magazines. Choose bright pictures in the same sorts of colours.

2 Glue the paper flowers all around the box and lid, so that they overlap a little and there is no space left.

3 Let the paper and glue dry completely, then paint the box and lid with clear varnish and leave them to dry.

Wrapping a rectangular present

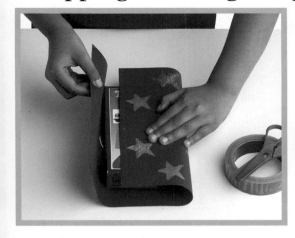

1 Put the present on a big sheet of paper. Fold the sides over the present so that they overlap and then tape them together.

2 Fold down the edge of the paper to cover one end of the present. Fold in the flaps at each side, so that they lie flat.

3 Fold in the pointed flap of paper and tape it down. Turn the present round and fold in the other end in the same way.

Wrapping a tubular present

1 Cut a long strip of paper, wider than the present. Roll the present in the paper, to make a tube and tape down the top edge.

2 Fold the paper down at one end of the tube. Pleat the rest of the paper down around it and tape it down.

3 Turn the tube around and fold the paper down in pleats, as before. Then tape the paper in position.

Wrapping a round present

1 Stand the present on two sheets of tissue paper. Pull the paper up over the present and cut it into a square, as shown.

2 Fold the paper up over the present and hold it with one hand. Squeeze the paper in tightly and secure it with sticky tape.

3 Cut a length of matching ribbon and cut points in the ends. Then tie it over the sticky tape in a big bow.

47

HAPPY CHRISTMAS

And here are the finished presents! To add the last touches, tie them in ribbons and attach a gift tag to each one.

Star-stencilled paper

RIBBONS AND BOWS
Tie the presents in ribbons that contrast with the wrapping paper. Some will look better with wide ribbons, and others with narrow ones.

Narrow gold ribbon

Angel-stencilled tissue paper

Wide gold ribbon bow

Blue box with lid decorated with cutouts

Contrasting purple ribbon

Box decorated with red and yellow cutouts

Gift tag attached with a red ribbon

Wax and paint paper tied with a red ribbon